Where, How and Why
to

BUY REAL ESTATE BEFORE <u>2009</u>

by Andrew R. Garvey

©

i

Although the author has exhaustively researched all sources and information contained in this book, neither he nor Garvey Publishing, LLC assumes any responsibility for errors, inaccuracies, omissions, or any other inconsistency herein. Any slights against people or organizations are unintentional. Neither the publisher nor the author is engaged in rendering legal, accounting, tax, or other professional services. Parties investing in real estate for themselves and/or other parties should use qualified, local real estate guidance and consult an attorney and/or accountant for specific applications to their real estate ventures.

Printed in the United States of America

Cover art by Christy Tucker

Copyright © 2003 by Garvey Publishing, LLC
Library of Congress Control Number: 2003095727
ISBN: 0-9743721-0-2

ATTENTION REAL ESTATE OFFICES, SALESPER-SONS, BROKERS AND CORPORATIONS: This book can increase customer and client loyalty when given as a gift, and can boost your listings and sales in the types of towns and regions recommended by this book. Quantity discounts are available by contacting Garvey Publishing, LLC, 1081 S. Glendale, Wichita, KS 67218

For my grandparents, Harry and Marion Hicks,
whose faith in me never faltered.

Special thanks to:
*Mom and Dad
*The two best REALTORS® I know, Rolf Westphal
with Century 21 in International Falls, MN and Uta
Hardy with Anchor Realty in Apalachicola, FL. Thanks
for all your advice and help with the book.
*Elton Parsons, Dennis Fitzroy and the whole Builders,
Inc. team
* My best friend, Atlas

TABLE OF CONTENTS

Introduction:

Baby Boomers are starting to reach the age at which they begin their lives as retirees. Nothing can alter the progression of time and the looming release of these individuals from the work force. Unlike momentary downturns and fleeting trends in the stock market, the Baby Boomers' trend towards retirement is a certainty and will technically continue until 2029 although mostly leveling off before 2020.

The wealthiest segment of the Baby Boomers will be retired by 2009. A significant percentage of the rest will have already bought a second or vacation home by then, since the number of potential purchasers qualified by income is expected to more than double between 2003-2009. Now is the time to buy real estate in the areas where these transitioning Baby Boomers will be moving.

The generation born between and including 1946 and 1964 are THE wealthiest group of up-and-coming retirees the world has ever seen. The booming 1990's economy was due in no small part to that dynamic generation working at their peak productivity during the prime of their careers. Additionally, they have been more conservative and intelligent with their investment strategies, unlike the naturally more impulsive, shortsighted, younger generations of American consumers. The Baby Boomers have, as a whole, done well for themselves by looking to the long-term for their individual security and not being foolish with their spending habits. They, an entire 76 million people at 28% of the population, are beginning to embark on the leisurely adventure that is life as a retired person.

As the Baby Boomers increase the demand for real estate in the college towns and growing resort areas to which they are migrating, the prices of the properties are following suit. Many areas of the country have booming real estate markets due to this trend, and the escalation of prices will only continue as time moves on its direct course.

And these areas are already growing rapidly. For example, a boomer friend of mine I've done business with recently bought several acres of land with 300+ feet of lake frontage in a growing resort town in Minnesota for $50,000 in cash and property. Two months and a new surveyors plat later, he sold one-third of that property for $55,000. Another third is currently listed at a market-supported $89,900, and he expects to gross around $100,000 for the final parcel. All told, he will likely quadruple his initial investment within two or three years. These are the sorts of profits that can be made in real estate before 2009.

As a licensed real estate professional in a growing field, my job is to help individuals, businesses and private trusts see large returns like these on their property investments in specific college towns and growing resort areas. Counseling others on real estate investing is what I do for a living, and this book is a simpler way of helping even more people prosper by my own experience on the ground researching the profit potential of these places. Oftentimes, real estate consultants and counselors charge up to $1,000 per day for doing the kind of work outlined in this manual. You, dear reader, have made a sensible investment already by buying my book.

During the course of your reading, you will learn where, how and why to buy real estate in areas where Baby Boomers and others will be buying vacation homes, pre-retirement properties and retirement homes before 2009 in order to show you a 10-30% *or more* annual rate of value appreciation on your investment. And I hope it will open your eyes to the real estate opportunities all across the country so that you, too, can someday retire with ease and comfort.

Section I

Chapter 1

Throughout the history of America, populations have periodically changed their locations en masse, bringing revenue and prosperity to wherever they settled.

In the very beginning of European migration to this country, Pilgrims braved the Atlantic by the thousands to colonize this new, vast land of freedom and economic opportunity. As their numbers increased, they swelled the towns and farmed the earth outside population centers, planting firmly both in the ground and in their minds the value of the land they occupied. The initial colonization was the very first American population shift, and it introduced the concept of individual land ownership to this continent.

The second population shift was encapsulated within the westward expansion as it continued until the late 1800's. Pioneers migrated across the uncharted, untraveled landscape to lay their claims, to herd cattle, to farm the land, and to achieve survival and prosperity for themselves and their families in any way they could.

The third American population shift was in the middle and late 1800's as the Industrial Revolution took hold. During this time, the population of America began to move from the sparsely populated rural areas of the country to concentrate in the cities. Cities were THE places to go for stable employment and they enabled the ambitious to make greater amounts of money than on a farm. Moving to the cities was the American dream during the Industrial Revolution, and this shift continued through World War I.

After World War II the government rewarded both it's fighting men and the families who supported them by establishing the first long-term, federally insured home loans. When that happened, the American population eagerly shifted from the crowded cities and inner-cities to congregate in newly established neighborhoods of single family homes, soon identified as the "suburbs." That fourth population shift thrived for over half a century and continues today but is losing many of its numbers to the next migration.

In the early 1980's we entered the beginning of the fifth American population shift, a movement from the suburbs to the "exurbs" (rural areas of the country) and it is thought that this massive movement to "exurbia" will continue for a number of decades.

National census figures, states' economic statistics, common sense, and an eye for trends in real estate are all pointing the common man, businesses, researchers, and real estate investors the way out of cities and out of suburbs to the exurbs.

In the 1990's, for the first time in six decades, rural areas of the country grew at a faster rate than urban and suburban areas. The nineties were when the fifth American migration began to attract attention.

But what's motivating this growing trend?

Factors such as the internet have enabled people to work from home without ever having to travel anywhere near an urban office. In 1990, 3% of the work force worked from home. By 1997, that number had risen to a full 7%. Home-based businesses currently represent a $1 trillion business market and employ 50 million people. Because of the internet, fax machines, cell phones, affordable home computers, etc., we are finding both young and older professionals operating from their homes in the mountains of Vermont, the beaches of Florida, the deserts of the Southwest, the forests of Washington, and the islands of Minnesota's ten thousand lakes. Many workers are no longer tied to an office, so often they enjoy the pleasures of working in more remote locations.

In these finance-conscious times, many people and companies are finding that land, housing, services and taxes are all usually much less expensive in exurbia. There is good research showing that many people are moving to exurbia to reap these financial benefits as well as hoping to provide a better education and a wholesome small-town atmosphere for their children. Large companies are finding it advantageous to set up shop in small towns and pump money into the village's cultural centers and historic sites in exchange for acquiring financial benefits and a new, marketable identity synonymous with that of small-town America.

The threat of terrorism is also pushing people away from large cities to less populated areas. We all saw what happened to the mind set of metropolitan residents after 9/11/01. New York State lost 252,000 people between April of 2001 and July of 2002, most of them leaving New York City and its suburbs. Terrorists have targeted densely populated areas, and it appears that many Americans are wanting to remove themselves and their families from high-density areas because of that possibility.

Put these factors together along with the fact that 76 million Baby Boomers are starting to retire with the money they've saved in their lifetimes (add to that an estimated **$8 trillion** in inheritance cash and property they'll acquire from their Depression-era parents in the next decade, according to the Boston Globe), and you've got some fairly accurate reasons for the population shifting to different parts of exurbia, namely growing resort areas.

In addition to quality resort areas, many college towns are also seeing considerable growth from this segment of the population. The value appreciation of college towns is due to different factors which I will touch on later.

Land is historically the most stable asset possible. No one is making any more of it. Many investors are putting their former stock market money into the hard asset of real estate that they can enjoy and feel confident about. Hard assets like vacant land do not usually lose value, whereas many stock market investors can lose money within seconds on both good and bad stocks. Most of us know people who lost up to and beyond 33% of their stocks' value in the first three years of the new millennium. It's up in the air as to how the stock market will do in the future, but in the recent past the market has been insecure and unstable due to human corruption and bad accounting inevitable in such a complex system, the irrational exuberance of the late 1990's, the terrorist attacks of 9-11-01, and diverse political factors and failures. At the time of printing, many investors are liquidating parts of their stock market portfolio after recouping some of their losses and are buying property where they can vacation or live full-time without worrying about losing value.

My work typically focuses on the profit potential of growing resort areas where vacant plots of residential land in prime locations can be purchased, minimally enhanced to boost their market value, and sold off relatively quickly. A reasonably quick, profitable turnaround on these properties is my primary focus and goal. However, *you* can always let your money sit in this land for several years if the area is a good one and if you don't need to pay off a loan.

The reasons for buying vacant parcels follow:

- Vacant land has lower taxes than land with structures.

- Insurance isn't necessary with vacant land.

- Land of this sort is easy to improve (clearing brush, building docks, etc.)

- Your prime market of second-home buyers and retirees like to design and build their own houses to fit vacant land

Depending on your needs and your investment plan, you may have to buy a piece of land with a house on it. This can be a good thing if you need somewhere to live as well as a place to put your money. There are also advantages to buying a house that you would not otherwise get with vacant land, specifically capital gains exclusions that I will touch on later.

Many land investors and speculators do not have their real estate licenses and indeed, it is not necessary that you have one. I would recommend, though, that your first step (if you are interested in a 10-30% or more annual value appreciation on your investment) is to at least take the classes that would enable you to get your real estate license, whether or not you actually take the test. Any real estate class you take will make you better informed about trade terminology, real estate law, and the financial aspects of real estate (financing, mortgages, taxes, etc.). Additionally, real estate law varies from state to state, so there may be any number of difficulties specific to the state you're working in that will not be touched on in this book.

Getting your actual real estate license can be either good or bad for you. There have certainly been times when I wished I did not have mine because as a licensed real estate professional I'm held to a higher code of ethics during any interaction and I need to disclose to the people I deal with that I'm licensed. That disclosure makes many people suspicious. A real estate agent also has more liability if he or she accidentally misrepresents a situation or position. Someone without a license does not have nearly as much liability.

Getting your real estate license leaves you tested on relevant information and open to earning commissions or referral fees on the property you research, which lowers your costs. I recommend that you at least take a real estate class through a trade education service or college before using the investment methods in this book.

The advice this book dispenses regarding researching and choosing real estate in these specific areas is hinged on the concept that if YOU like it, then hopefully others in the region with financial clout will also like it and create a continuing demand until 2009 and beyond. We all know how people from New York and New Jersey enjoy vacationing or having a second home in coastal Maine or mountainous Vermont. People from Georgia and other Southern states tend to travel to Florida for swimsuit vacations on sandy beaches and many already have second homes along its' coasts.

People like nice areas that are close by where they can breathe the night air of the mountains, hear crickets chirping in the silence of the hills, or feel the spray of waves crashing on the beach. Most people appreciate the same timeless human moments, so if you like the area, chances are that others in your region will too.

After all, who isn't going to pay money to live in an area where they cross a wooden bridge across a river on the way to the grocery store? Who doesn't like living where they can enjoy the smell of wood smoke from a mountain cabin, see wispy clouds brushed on an open sky, or watch lobster boats inching across the horizon of the bay?

Ideally, this book will help you find the scene in America you most want to occupy and show you how to buy and sell it for profit while enjoying it between transactions. You will be looking for property where people can make memories easily because places that make memories also make money. Your goal is to see value appreciation of 10-30% *or more* annually on real estate in specific, desirable areas without doing much or anything to the land.

Here's how.

Chapter 2:

"How do I find the areas that have a good rate of market value appreciation?"

The procedures to follow for finding speculative real estate will vary depending on your location, your financial situation, and the type of investment property in which you're interested.

First of all it's best to invest in real estate near where you live. The closer the property, the easier it is to check up on it and the simpler it is to do research in the first place. In other words, it's probably not feasible to research or buy real estate in Florida if you live in Oregon, unless you have a private jet or frequent flier miles to burn. If people do engage in long-distance investing, they often have a consultant or counselor on the ground doing their research for them so they don't have to.

Some regions of the country are not a natural draw for a national, regional, or state vacation crowd, necessitating real estate research outside of one's comfort zone. If you live in Salina, Kansas, for instance, you might need to travel as far as the Ozarks of Missouri or the mountains of Colorado before you encounter a suitable area for speculative real estate investment before 2009.

Usually, though, you most likely will need to stay near to where you live.

When researching property, you would do best to keep in mind a basic rule of economics. . .

"There must be demand to sell a product."

This should be fairly self-explanatory. If you buy property in a remote location that's inaccessible or unknown to most people but think that it has completely untapped potential and that most people would love it if only they saw it, you probably won't make much or any money on that parcel. America is a big, beautiful place with many undiscovered nooks and crannies in every region, and I've personally experienced these places and been humbled by their beauty many times before financial common sense kicked in and I turned down the "opportunity." I can't tell you how many times I've heard of other people falling in love with an isolated area and actually buying several 40-acre parcels of remote forest, foolishly thinking they will be able to turn around in a few years and sell the property in the Wall Street Journal® for 500 times what they paid for it to some faceless millionaire who signs blank checks and buys land without getting an appraisal first.

Well, wealthy people aren't typically that dumb. They usually enter the halls of financial power by being fairly shrewd in the first place. There is very little chance that you can make a remote, inaccessible (but beautiful) piece of property appeal to a very small segment of the population, so it's usually best to stick with properties close to civilization and amenities that the middle to upper-middle classes can afford.

Side Note: Some states have a specific appeal for potential buyers of high-end properties. The states of Florida, Texas, Iowa, South Dakota, and Kansas all have a clause in their homestead laws that exempts the owner from forfeiting his or her home if they declare bankruptcy. Florida is probably the most famous state where this is the case, since many actors and businessmen have avoided creditors by building multi-million-dollar homes that they were allowed to keep after declaring bankruptcy. People such as Scott Sullivan, the CFO for WorldCom, Burt Reynolds, OJ Simpson, and Dennis Kozlowski of Tyco® International have all had estates in Florida unable to be touched by the bankruptcy process. For the wealthy (most of whom are actually scrupulous, responsible individuals), desireable areas in these states, particularly in Florida, have high demand.

A different and equally interesting law is on the books for Florida, Nevada, Texas, Washington, and Wyoming. In those states, there is no such thing as a state income tax. If you live in those states and you're investing in speculative real estate you will still have to pay property taxes but you're lucky enough to be excluded from paying state income taxes.

Your best option is to find areas near metropolises that have already begun to be developed and moved into by people from those large cities because there's a much larger consumer base for vacation retreats or second homes near cities. There will be more demand for those properties since there's less drive time, pushing the prices higher. The more demand there is for certain properties, the more the prices climb.

A good rule of thumb for choosing an area outside of a city to research is this: People usually want vacation properties at least two hours outside of any major city to avoid traffic, noise, and light pollution, but are usually only willing to sit in a car for up to six hours before hating a vacation weekend that hasn't yet started. Six hours one way, six hours back, and they've wasted the sunlight of an entire vacation day. Few people want to waste that much time. In other words, you should usually look for areas between <u>two</u> and <u>six</u> hours of drive time from the closest metropolitan area.

That rule doesn't work all the time, though. For instance, Atlanta, Georgia is around seven hours from the closest port or bay on the Gulf Coast. And yet, roughly 25% of the people now buying beach front or beach access homes in that area are from Atlanta and its suburbs, due in part to inexpensive airline flights, a factor you can't always count on to bring people to an area of regional or extra-regional growth.

Assuming you aren't from Atlanta, look on a map of the closest metropolitan area near you and trace several circles encompassing 2,3,4,5, or even 6 hour drive times on all sides. Then look inside these circles and see if you recognize any familiar mountains, ski areas, tourist attractions, oceans, or lakes.

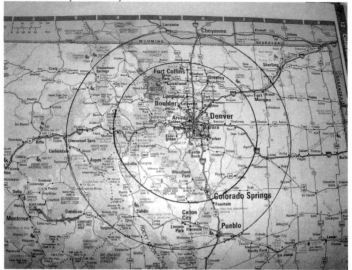

Drive times will vary in your circle. In this case, Vail is almost 2 hours outside Denver, but Colorado Springs is 1 hour, 15 mins. I also skewed the circles towards the mountains, the destination of choice in Colorado.

Author's Note: Water has a timeless, hypnotic quality that appeals to people. For whatever reasons, it is very comforting sitting next to a lake, on the bank of a river, or in the surf of an ocean. In real estate, as in life, water is a reason in itself. If you find an area with a nice body of water that attracts boaters, fishermen, tourists, and seasonal residents, you might have found a place that will grow quickly and boost property values.

Once you've jotted down a few locations within these circles where you think or know that numbers of people enjoy visiting (because all people who buy property visit as sightseers and tourists first), pick up the

the phone, get on the internet, and start communicating with the real estate agents in these areas.

Usually it's best to talk to about three agents in each town because it's possible you've talked to a rookie who doesn't know the place like someone who's lived there his whole life. And never agree to sign a single-agent buyers agreement with any agent you talk to, especially not this soon. I'll explain why in Chapter 5.

The first question to ask is this: "Are you seeing much property value appreciation in your area?"

The agent will either start exclaiming about how the area is booming, OR they'll make you repeat the question and comment that their area offers beautiful vistas or something else that isn't an answer to the

Side Note: I have talked in this way to some agents who have rattled off the names of celebrities who live in the area, as though this implies that the area is a good investment opportunity. Celebrities mean nothing when researching speculative property, except in extremely rare instances like the real estate boom that occurred in Jackson Hole, Wyoming. Oftentimes, celebrities are hounded by the press and paparazzi so they may have bought property for the sole purpose of being isolated from the outside world. Last time I checked, undeveloped, inaccessible areas of the country weren't a big draw for my primary market of vacationers or retirees. Celebrities are not necessarily a good value indicator, they are just an appealing idea thrown out by agents wanting sales. Being close to popular people was a concern in high school, but as adults making investment decisions, we don't need to listen to this aspect of the realtor/middleman's pitch.

question you asked. There isn't much of a reason to dally on the line with the latter, because you want land that is going up in value without doing anything to it.

If the agent has said that average land values are going up anywhere from 10% to 30% per year, then that area might be a place you want to put your money. Any higher than 30% per year, and you should immediately drop everything you're doing, hop in your car, and go look at the place. Higher than 30% average is an amazing degree of value appreciation, and finding it is rare. However, I have found that when a realtor says that the average is 25-30% annual appreciation, there are specific properties from which you can see much more market value increases than those stated.

Real World Example:

Extraordinary cases of value appreciation occur more often than one might think. A favorite example is in Port St. Joe, Florida, where an interior lot (a lot without a view of the beach, but within close walking distance to it) in a new development sold for $90,000 in November of 2001. By August of 2002, the same type of lot was selling for up to $425,000, a 355% value appreciation inside of ten months.

Amazing cases like this exist, and this one happened in an area where there was a 25-30% average annual appreciation rate already. This example DID have a special factor involved, specifically, the closing of a paper mill nearby. That made the area more desirable because there was no longer a sweaty-gym-sock smell drifting across the beach.

The Florida panhandle in general has historically been known as "The Redneck Riviera" because of the fishing industry and the blue-collar demographic. It's undergoing a large identity shift now, as the St. Joe Company® (the largest private landowner in Florida with over a million acres) is working with one of its subsidiaries (Arvida®), and a former Disney® development head to remake the entire region into, "The Great Northwest." They also have the funds needed to do it, since they are developing or in the planning stages of developing seven large subdivisions simultaneously along the panhandle of Florida and several more elsewhere, planning for a large influx of Baby Boomers to Florida wanting second and pre-retirement homes in college towns and growing resort areas until 2009 and beyond. The area is getting a lot of national press right now, the developments and golf courses necessary to make new resort areas are under construction, and the beaches are some of the best in America. There's even a $200 million international airport expected to be constructed in Panama City that could be larger than Tampa's. It's a very hot area for real estate right now, but if you choose to investigate in the panhandle (or anywhere else), watch out for real estate bubbles, because they may exist! Always do your research!!

Whenever large developers get involved in an area, the property values go up, sometimes drastically. In parts of the Florida panhandle, property values have soared in the last ten years, and could continue to go up in the future.

After having the question about property value appreciation answered in the affirmative, you need to find out the following about the area:

19

-The approximate average price of a <u>single-family home</u> in a prime location for value appreciation.

-The approximate average price of a <u>vacant residential lot</u> in a prime location for value appreciation.

-The approximate average price of a <u>forty acre parcel</u> in or near a prime location for value appreciation.

The answers to these questions will help you determine the areas that fall most in accordance with the price you want to spend on any given property. If an area is completely out of your price range, simply move on and call the REALTORS® in the next town or city on your list.

If you have succeeded in finding an area near you where the real estate agents agree that there are large percentages of value gained every year, plan a week to get away and investigate the area if the property values are in your price range or the range in which you can borrow. This is where the fun begins.

Chapter 2 1/2: An Easy Way to Research.

After you've found an area with potential, you can always talk to a private real estate appraiser in the area to recommend suitable properties for optimal return. Determining the value of properties based partly on the current market value appreciation is what appraisers do for a living, and local ones should know the area fairly well. They don't come tremendously cheap, however, and their advice is rarely, if ever, free. Their counsel can usually be retained for a few hundred dollars.

It is best to use a mixture of appraiser advice and personal research in order to make good and proper decisions. If you are looking for property in which to invest a substantial portion of your savings, I think that it is extremely important that you do a degree of your own research so that you're not just trusting someone elses' word about what to do with *your* money. And there's never anything wrong with being well-informed.

Authors Note: Bubbles exist. As in any national trend (the stock market, Cabbage Patch dolls, etc.), real estate speculation will create pockets of erroneously inflated prices. The only way to find out if the place is seeing a false real estate value bubble is to be on the ground researching the area. Time spent talking to real estate professionals, appraisers, and the common man will help determine if you are involved in a price bubble. If it is a bubble, chances are that there won't be much construction of houses going on, since it will be mostly speculators holding vacant land and maybe just subdividing it. Looking for new construction will help you determine whether or not there is a bubble, although bubbles can exist even throughout any area, construction or not.

What you can do to research an area follows in the next chapter.

Chapter 3: Firsthand research.

"I'm here. Now what do I do?"

First of all, try to do your firsthand research out of season. There are several reasons for this, one of which is that fewer offers are made on listed properties during the off-season, so you might be able to get a good deal from a desperate landowner.

Another reason to shop for properties during the off-season is that you will be able to get better rates on your hotel or motel. (An insignificant fact, perhaps, but it comes in handy if you are doing a lot of research.)

Yet another reason is that you will be able to see the locals in their real state of being, without pretense or vested opinions, and those are the sorts of locals from whom I prefer to get local information. They're almost too honest about the area and the tourists, and they tell you what they think about EVERYTHING.

(If you have trouble during the off-season imagining what the area looks like during the nicer months, just take a look at the local postcards.)

Once in the town, start enjoying your time there. Park your car, visit the chamber of commerce, and start shopping in the downtown area. Buy a coffee from the local roaster, buy some postcards. And while you're doing all this, casually ask the employees and people you run into if they know anything about real estate in the area.

You will find that some of the best information can come from talking to the full-time residents. They have local knowledge and local connections and can refer you to reputable REALTORS®, appraisers who know the area, and news of what's going on in the local business community. Any sort of information you can cull from them is potentially helpful, and it's often better than knowledge you will get from someone with a financial interest in your investment money. After all, a REALTOR® isn't going to want to tell you that his town has been slated to be turned into a county trash dump. The locals will tell you that.

However, it's important that you also take local information with a grain of salt. If an area has a booming real estate market and properties are in that 10-30% annual appreciation range, a true local might tell you not to buy property there. He or she might say things like:

"Man, them prices is way too high. No one's gonna pay that."

"Hell, that land ain't good huntin'."

"Don't buy land here. [Because my property taxes are killing me!]"

Despite the informational pros and cons while talking to the locals, you will soon start to see trends of thinking in that area. Keep your eyes and ears open and don't get so overwhelmed with money-making possibilities that you talk too much. There's a reason why good real estate researchers have two eyes and two ears but only one mouth.

Real World Example:

While researching lakefront land in Minnesota, I drove by a house that had a big, orange spray-painted sign in the front yard. It said, "Don't buy from —— —— Realty."

When I asked the REALTOR® I was talking with (who was thankfully from a different office) he said that real estate office hadn't disclosed to that particular buyer that his well water was contaminated with lethal levels of various poisons. Meanwhile, the owner's young family had been drinking the water for two months before they had an independent test done.

I decided then and there to never talk with that office. They weren't just unethical, they committed a crime. I don't want to work with criminals.

Look into every little lead that you come across while researching an area. It could save you money. . . or your life.

After getting an initial feel for the town and the locals, start driving around in the areas that you have heard might be a good place to buy property. This stage of the research will take some time.

On a note pad, keep a list of streets on which property has potential. For instance, if you are looking at an area that has a lake, note the names of the streets that run by properties on that lake. The same is true if there is an ocean nearby. If you are in an area that has ski resorts, neighborhoods close to the slopes or near a highway leading to the ski area should be researched.

If you are looking at an area that doesn't have water or ski slopes, simply look at the general condition of the area and the homes. Often, trailer homes and RV's are a signal that the neighborhood is not a good opportunity. HOWEVER, you shouldn't always immediately discount the possibility of buying property near trailer parks and cinder-block homes. Some of the best deals can be made on land with ugly structures simply because it's cheaper, and the surrounding area might be escalating in value quite quickly. I have, in fact, seen areas where new, four-story mansions are built directly adjacent to rusted trailer homes leveled by sheets of broken plywood. Real estate in some regions gets pretty crazy, so always make sure you know your area before you put money into real estate.

Two houses on the Gulf coast. One is fairly new and up to code, the other is made of cinderblock and was probably grandfathered in. The really interesting thing about this picture is that both are probably of comparable value since houses in this area don't add much value to the expensive price of the land itself.

On a separate note pad, jot down the properties that have "For Sale" signs, the addresses, and the name of the REALTOR®. The information you take down now will help to determine the value of land in that area later. You may even take pictures with a digital camera in order to remember what the place looks like. This is especially helpful if you are not already familiar with the area.

Once this is completed and you have a good feel for the place (it may take a few days), go to the courthouse with a detail map and your notes in hand.

Side Note: If you have found an area where it looks as though most lots are built on, but then come across a large, undeveloped piece of land in the correct area, take notes on where it is and what it is near. This way, when you next go to the courthouse, you will have the ability to find out on a plat map who owns it and if it suits you, contact them and make an offer. In other words, be on the lookout for brush-filled, overgrown land that *doesn't* catch your eye because you might be able to buy it at a good price.

Oftentimes people hold onto their land for sentimental reasons or habit. They'll pay the property taxes once a year, yet never do anything with it because they entertain the idea in their heads that it'll come in handy for something at some point. Occasionally, you will find one of these absentee landowners owning larger tracts of land exactly where you have been looking for speculative real estate. It is always easy to call them up and ask them if they are willing to sell the land, and many times they will be interested, but nothing speaks louder than a written contract with earnest money.

A seller can always toy around with the idea of selling their land, but that's just what it is. . . an idea. Once an offer to buy is in writing on a piece of paper they can hold in their hands, the owner can count the 0's in the cash amount and realize that he can have that much tangible money in his pocket just by signing his name.

If you want to buy a piece of land that isn't listed with a REALTOR® or even for sale, talking to the person about selling it is okay but it's probably mostly a waste of your time until he sees cash on the barrel head.

Chapter 4: The County Courthouse

Your first stop in the courthouse is at the county tax assessors office.

If the courthouse is a small and intimate place, walk in and introduce yourself as someone who was looking into property in the area for personal investment reasons. Never lie, but it is essential that you do not appear as though you have ample finances or work for a large company. [Often these towns are fairly small, and if an outsider comes in at the behest of a corporation or group of investors wanting to put some of their assets into land in the area, word will get around and you will run into nothing but roadblocks and cold shoulders. People in general resist change, so the citizenry might not appreciate your interest no matter how much money you bring to the community.]

Real World Example:

I was researching land in Minnesota again last year and I made the mistake of telling a particularly entrepreneurial tavern owner that I worked for some people who could help out the prosperity of the town, and that he and I might be "seeing a lot of each other in the future."

I meant nothing by this except to imply that his many businesses and my investors would probably cross paths in the future as he was ambitious about turning that particular small town into an even larger tourist destination via his many PR campaigns and I had assumed that my clients would at some point meet him simply by grace of proximity.

He almost beat me up.

"What makes you think that you can breeze in here and be all mysterious like that? Saying weird things and not explaining them! Who do you work for?!!" he ended up shouting as he backed me into a corner.

Apparently, an extremely sensitive political situation had been going on that concerned him, and he actually thought that I was a hired spy for the Senator-to-be.

To convince him that I wasn't a political "spy," I had to take my shirt off to show him I wasn't wearing a wire. I'm not kidding. I could either take my shirt off, or walk away with a black eye and a bad name.

Be careful what you say in a small town, because even the most innocent comment can get you in a lot of trouble. I'm serious. People get crazy.

Another time I needed to keep my mouth shut (which I did this time) was in a small town on the Gulf coast where the town council was less than encouraging of new businesses and out-of-towners moving to the area. This group of good ol' boys was always trying to put a stop to new sewer projects and developments because they wanted to keep things in the town as they had always been (i.e. trailer parks, crippled roadways, no economic future, etc.). They were the cliche of country-folk suspicious of new ideas and outsiders. But people were moving to their area because of the views, the weather, the coast, and the low taxes. In order to prevent suspicion of my motives or background, I did my general research wearing jeans, a dirty t-shirt, and a beard and made a concerted effort to not sound too educated.

In some small towns the name of the game is "low profile."

You might be getting the idea by now that researching land for speculative purposes can be something of an adventure. If you think that, that means I'm reproducing the feeling I have about it. It is an adventure.

Think for a second about what you're doing. After all, you're often coming to a rural town populated by good ol' boys and buying their property for a fair price with the intent of selling it for much more in a few years or less. It has an undercurrent of something that strikes of hidden agendas and uncommon knowledge and if you buy the right property at the right time, you will make plenty of money at it. What's more adventureous than that?

Often the citizens of the town can't pay their speedily rising property taxes anymore and they need someone to take the property off their hands before they declare bankruptcy. A good speculator will buy property from them for a fairly good price the owner never dreamed of and then sell it for much more within a few short years. Both people usually win but as soon as you intimate that you have access to large resources, people become suspicious and think they got a bad deal. Stay QUIET and LIKABLE, or just plain ANONYMOUS.

The best way to go about researching a certain area if you're an individual investor with no background to keep silent is to simply go slowly and make friends in the town. There's nothing like being invited to dinner to help you better understand the power structure of the town and to find out who makes the real decisions that will affect you as a property owner.

Back to the county courthouse. . .

At the assessors office, ask to take a look at the CRV's (Certificates of Real estate Value) for the area that you have pinpointed as being a prime location for value appreciation. [I use "CRV" as a completely generic term for convenience because the name of the form actually depends on the state. Every state where I've researched property has its own form where they record sales prices. If they don't have papers like these, they will probably have it on computer which will save you time and effort.] If they ask why you want to see these forms, don't reply with a haughty remark such as, "Well, they're public records, aren't they?" That will make people try really hard to *not* help you.

The best way to respond (as I mentioned before) is to reply that you are looking for a place to get away and the area seemed suitable, but you wanted to make sure that the area had good investment potential before you purchased property. More often than not this should suffice since the rituals of bureaucratic routine generally dull employees' sense of curiosity, and yours is probably a truthful answer anyway.

CRV's —or the appropriate form, depending on the state— are usually filed by the year. Begin at least five years back, if not more. The more history you have regarding sales prices, the better you can predict your ROI (Return On Investment). The purpose of the CRV's is to record the sales prices for the properties in the county in order to establish appropriate property taxes. So if they don't have CRV's, ask for the form on which they record the location and price of yearly property sales. Then, to be friendly, ask how they got so "blessed" as to live in such a wonderful area. Don't spend too long talking to the people, though, because you've got work to do.

Side Note: City Hall

City Hall is often useless when compiling information since they don't record the really relevant facts and figures, unless they have an ECONOMIC

34

DEVELOPMENT COUNCIL. Many times, towns are small enough that they might not have one of these offices, but this is <u>always</u> the first place to go to do your research.

The economic development council's primary job is to bring individuals, businesses and industry to their city and to supply information to any interested parties about local economic conditions, tourism, etc., in order to try enhancing the area's economy. If the town or city has an economic development council, they are required to help you find all the information about the city that you request, and they will have much of it right at hand.

The planning and zoning commission might also be of interest to you regarding new home starts, new neighborhoods, etc., so that's another place in city hall that might be worth a visit.

Once you have the CRV's in hand, first find the address on the form and make sure it lies within your optimal target area by cross checking it with your notes you took the day before and the map you brought in with you. Chances are that most properties won't be in the areas you marked, but you will get accustomed to skimming through these papers quickly.

Once you have found a CRV that has the appropriate address, look at the rest of the form to make sure that:

1. The buyer and seller weren't relatives or related businesses

2. The property wasn't a gift or inheritance

3. A transaction wasn't involved in the trade of property

4. The buyer wasn't a religious or charitable organization

5. The buyer wasn't a unit of government

6. The transaction wasn't due to condemnation or foreclosure

7. There wasn't a payoff or resale of the contract

8. A name wasn't added to or a co-owner's name removed from the deed

9. The buyer didn't purchase a partial interest only

10. The purchase agreement wasn't signed over two years before.

These ten reasons above have the potential of affecting the accuracy of the sales price, so you don't want to record those. Usually, if any of these instances occurred, there will be a simple box that is checked to accept or deny that specific transaction's inclusion in the assessor's survey to determine property taxes.

Now that you've found a form that matches your criteria, find out on the form whether the property was a house, a vacant lot, or larger acreage. Then write down the sales price for the house, lot or acreage in it's own property-type column for that year, and find the next CRV that fits your criteria.(see asterisk * p.38)

When you have the CRV's for the desired area and property type for a specific year written into a column, ask for the CRV's for the next year, and do the same for them. Then take one year's prices and add them together. Divide the sum by the number of entries you added for the total.

This will give you the average yearly sales price for a piece of property in the area you desire. Do the same with the next year's list, and so on.

Example

Sales Prices for 2000 (from CRV's)

Vacant, one-acre lots only

1)	**$25,470**
2)	**$38,880**
3)	**$36,439**
4)	**$57,440**
5)	**$17,860**
6)	**$23,500**
7)	**+ $72,390**

$271,979 = Total cost of vacant, one acre lots in prime areas sold in 2000.

Then divide your total by the number of entries you added to get that total. In this case, there were **7** entries.

$271,979 / 7 = $38,854.14

$38,854.14 is your average price for a vacant lot in 2000.

Step #2:

Once you have acquired the averages of property for several years in a row, you can find the average annual value appreciation.

Average prices for vacant lots in subsequent years:

2000 = $38,854 | From 2000 to 2001, the average
2001 = $51,764 | price for a vacant lot went up 33%
2002 = $64,612 | 2001 to 2002 = 24%
2003 = $71,343 | 2002 to 2003 = 10%

If you average these numbers, one acre lots in this area have gone up an average of 22% every year for the past three years.

All of these numbers and this process is a good way of trying to project with some accuracy what the real estate market could do in the future. Just add 22% onto 2003's average price for a vacant lot and you might be in the range you could expect the next year (barring any major crises in the economy). However, I recommend that you base your projections on information taken from a longer span of time than four years like in this abbreviated example.

Once you have the average sales prices for several years immediately previous to the point in time you occupy, compare the results and figure out the percentage appreciation per year. Doing this can help you chart your estimated profits and give you a good sense of current property values.

* When compiling any numbers at the county courthouse or elsewhere, it is **extremely important** that you find some sort of common denominator you can use to directly compare property values throughout the region and throughout the years. Good common denominators to use are 1)sales prices broken down into cost per acre, or 2)average price per running foot of water frontage. Using direct value-to-quantity ratios is invaluable for quick mental math and for relatively accurate estimates of property-specific value, both when

figuring current yearly averages on paper and projecting them forward, and when researching real estate in the field.

In addition to the county assessors office, you will want to browse the other departments and offices in the courthouse in search of relevant information. I always go to the environmental services department, the tax office, and wherever else I can find statistics about an area. Relevant information you might want to research could be:

* Population growth
* the area's tax base
* setbacks from water
* sewer accessibility
* areas of residential and commercial zoning
* new neighborhoods
* new business growth
* tourism statistics
. . . and the list goes on.

The leg work (trust me, it's fun)

Chapter 5: Beyond the Courthouse:

Once you have compiled your numbers on the neighborhoods that show the greatest opportunity, it's time to drive around with several REALTORS® in order to look at specific properties.

Usually, it's never good to sign a single-agent buyer's agreement with any REALTOR®, no matter how likeable they are or how well they know the area.

Reasons not to sign a Buyer's Agreement:
  - If you buy any property in the area, even a FSBO, you will need to include that agent in the sale.
  - A Buyer's Agreement does not mean that the agent will do everything in his power to get you a better sales price. He still gets a percentage of

the sales price, so the more you pay, the more he gets.

- You will want to work with as many agents while researching property as you can. Working with one exclusively will limit the scope of your research, and therefore, your opportunities.

- Having a buyer's agent doing the research for you could make you lazy by depending on them instead of doing your own research.

Most real estate offices are part of a local MLS. An MLS is a "Multiple Listing Service," which means that if one office lists a property, another office can sell it and both offices split the commission. I would recommend that you drive around with at least three REALTORS®, because even though they will show you any property on the MLS, they all have different personalities, different perspectives, and different information. In Colorado, I once thought that a certain small town was a dud until I drove around with an agent who himself was doing land speculation and making money at it, he knew the history of the area, and the neighborhoods that showed the greatest land value appreciation. It's nice being surprised like that, and I learned for the first time that the town had been scouted by major developers as a possible golf community.

Author's Note: I have noticed in the areas I've researched that some people need a quick sale of their property, so they end up selling for less. Personal problems like divorces or creditor pressures- or even time constraints on a sale like those involved in 1031 exchanges- can make property owners sell their real estate quicker and for less money than if they were simply influenced by normal circumstances.

Obviously, it's sad when people specifically with money problems have to compromise their property's value potential in order to meet payment deadlines. In a 1031 exchange (I'll talk about these later), a person has a limited number of days in which to complete a sale and purchase. Everyone, at one time or another, has had to make sacrifices they didn't want to make. But when people need to sell their property, they will do what they have to do. When people are desperate, they need help and you may be able to help them, with some advantage to you.

A good way of finding out if you can help someone in need is to ask the REALTOR® how "motivated" the seller is. If the REALTOR® has gotten permission from a seller to let potential buyers know this information, then he is breaking no laws by answering. This can help you judge the flexibility of the potential purchase price and determine if you can get a good deal on the property while helping the seller out of a tough situation.

As you are driving around with your agents (always drive around with more than one, at separate times), ask about tourism and local attractions, where the tourists come from and how many there are in a season, what the locals do for fun, and find out if there are any golf courses in the area. As elitist as it sounds (I call it "realistic"), the presence of golf courses often indicates a higher-end vacation infrastructure, which is important if you want to make money there. Also ask about the presence of gated communities, because those are also indicative of a wealthier demographic.

Another good statistic to find out from your REALTOR® is the average cost per running foot of frontage on water. Typically, for waterfront land, the size of the parcel is less important than its' total amount of water frontage. I have seen areas where a gorgeous, two-acre parcel with 150 feet of water frontage was exactly the same price as a lot with 150 feet frontage but with only 150 feet to the road (depth). Water frontage is usually the most important value qualifier.

If you are in a growing resort area that has lakes, rivers, or oceans, you need to find out about several other factors specific to land near water. Your real estate agents can help answer your questions about the following, but always double-check at the courthouse what they say:

Flood Plains: Find out from the REALTOR® you are working with if the properties you are looking at are in a flood plain or a flood zone. Most times, land in an area that is low enough to be flooded has construction issues and insurance problems associated with it. Often you cannot build a structure in a flood zone, negating the need for flood insurance. If an individual is able to build there, he or she may have to raise the grade (height) of the land in the building site or put the structure on stilts. With either of these there will usually be restrictions on the type of insurance you can get. Some areas qualify for Federal Flood Insurance and if they do it can be beneficial for you although it doesn't say much about the area's weather. If a property is technically in a flood zone but isn't really in danger of flooding, you could get a local surveyor or engineer to re-shoot the elevations and get you a map amendment.

A map amendment (exclusion from the flood plain) will prevent you from having to pay for costly insurance, and will help the future sale of the property.

Docks: You may or may not be able to build a dock into the ocean, bay, or lake, depending on the level of control exerted by the various environmental agencies. Wetlands are usually a highly protected form of land since they are home to so many thousands of animal, plant, and insect species. As a result, docks for boats or fishing can be difficult to acquire permits for, although this, of course, depends on your area. You should ask your REALTOR® about dock length restrictions and laws governing the acquisition of a dock permit. Agents are there to answer questions, although you should always double-check for yourself what they say.

Sewerage and Gray Water Systems: Near lakes, rivers, streams, and oceans, septic, sewer, and gray water issues abound. If there is no access to a city sewer line, you will likely have restrictions on setbacks for a structure with a septic system. This is to keep the runoff far enough away from the shoreline to prevent contamination of the waterways. If you do have access to city sewer, a future building will probably be able to be closer to the shore.

Gray water runoff is a similar case, although it all depends on your area. Again, ask your REALTOR® for information, but always double-check it at the courthouse. If you want to spend the time, you may familiarize yourself with the basics of the Federal Clean Water Act.

Water Rights: In areas of the Southwest where humans expect to live normally in deserts, water rights are a huge issue. These places have restrictions on the amount of water that landowners can use, and there is a significant cost for purchasing water that already sits under the land or runs through it. If this is the case in the area you are researching, there will usually be a separate branch of the local government dedicated solely to the water rights issue. Private companies and water conservation organizations can also play a role in the governance and enactment of water rights legislation. Check around with whomever you can to find out about the specific case for your area.

Low Density Development: In some areas, the city, county, or developer felt there should be a limit on the number of people in an area so as to maintain a more pristine natural environment or to just ensure that the area doesn't get too crowded. To do this, the city or county will mandate laws governing the number of livable structures per acre (single family homes, condos, town homes, etc.) or require a specific amount of square footage coupled with water frontage in order to build a structure if the lot sizes are less than an acre. Check with the local planning and zoning authority for this sort of information.

A private developer can also limit the lot sizes in his development. These are difficult if not impossible to change, as they fall within the restrictive covenants of the neighborhood. Unless there is a majority landowner vote to change them, they will be unalterable. In other words, if you have seen 50 foot wide lots on the water, don't think that you can buy a lot with 150 feet of water frontage and break it up into three lots to sell individually, because you may not be able to. Always check on lot size restrictions off, near, or on the water.

Wells: Whether or not the property you are researching is near or on the water, you should always find out about your ability to drill a well on the property. Often you will find that the underlying rock is difficult to get a drill bit through, adding to the cost of the well-drilling. Other times, the water table is extremely far under the ground, which also adds to the cost of a new well since well drillers charge by the foot.

In some areas where the primary economic infrastructure is agricultural or industrial, the well water might be contaminated by chemicals and therefore unfit for drinking. Poisoned wells can also happen near trash dumps. Even certain kinds of trees or underground rock can produce naturally-occurring poisons that will contaminate your well water.

Some property owners that have well water issues like these have employed the use of water bladders under the house or underground cisterns that are filled occasionally by a water truck. I have even seen more holistic systems that funnel rainwater from the roof into cisterns for limited use in the home and garden, although in parts of the southwest these are actually illegal, for some reason. One would think that water conservation that showed this kind of initiative and ingenuity would be lauded, but that's sadly not the case. In other words, if you're in the parts of the southwest where this is illegal, make sure you let your rainwater evaporate so you won't get fined.

Chapter 6: College Towns:

College towns are the second type of area where real estate prices are escalating steadily in response to the increased demand by Baby Boomers. There are many reasons why Baby Boomers are moving to college towns, some of which include the arts' scene, concerts, quality retail shops, trendy bars and clubs, historic buildings and museums, public lectures by authors and the intelligentsia, and the ability to audit college classes for pleasure. It makes perfect sense to want to live where there is so much dynamic thought, culture, and entertainment in a fairly small area. Additionally, many adults have fond memories of college, so reestablishing contact with one's initial adult experience is a natural urge and brings full circle one of life's many cycles. I personally know many Baby Boomers who have created a new beginning for themselves in college towns where they joined art boards and book clubs, and they're some of the most happy, fulfilled, and cultured retired individuals I've met.

The real estate speculation market is a bit different in college towns, however. Because of the many different small neighborhoods in college towns that have their own subtle distinctions and flavors— sometimes changing every few hundred feet— you should talk to a local appraiser and get his or her advice about what you want to do. It's often too difficult for an outsider to pinpoint specific areas as the most desirable with the most potential for value appreciation in a college town.

A somewhat lucrative option for your money in real estate in college towns is to buy an old house or building in a prime location and rent out rooms to college students. The land under it is still going up in value and you're paying the taxes on the place with the rents you receive in addition to maybe earning some income. You may have run across the hundreds of books that explain how to make money by owning rental properties. While rental money can be a good income, it often is nowhere near the percentage of value appreciation you can see on vacant land in a booming area up until 2009. To rent out a building, you will encounter upkeep and maintenance issues, insurance difficulties, tenant problems, and all the other drawbacks of owning a piece of property where other people live. If this is the route for you, there are hundreds of books available online and in your local bookstore that deal specifically with making money on rental properties.

The Big Fish

Chapter 7: LLC's, Financing, Partnerships, Investors.

One option (perhaps the best) that many individuals, business partners, and couples are taking advantage of in order to purchase speculative real estate is to form a Limited Liability Company (LLC).

I would advise you to seek the counsel of your Certified Public Accountant and Attorney before setting up an LLC. The restrictions and advantages of LLC's vary between states and all aspects should be researched with your CPA even though LLC's are fairly easy to set up. You might be able to find in a bookstore a few legal books that walk you step-by-step through the process and the implications of starting an LLC in your state.

LLC's originated to combine the best aspects of a corporation with the tax advantages of a partnership, without the red tape of either. They came into existence for the first time with the Limited Liability Company Act of Wyoming in 1977 and eventually caught on nationwide. There are now LLC laws for all fifty states.

Essentially, LLC's limit personal liability if the company gets in legal trouble. With an LLC, creditors and lawsuits cannot go after the members' personal assets and cannot hold individual members responsible for the debts of the LLC.

If you feel particularly ambitious and confident in your ability to make money in speculative real estate, finding parties to invest in your LLC can be a lucrative option for you, since you will be able to charge management and maintenance fees, as well as receiving a percentage of the profits when you sell. This is a complicated operation, though, both legally and financially, and I recommend that you consult your CPA and lawyer before operating an LLC full-time in this way. After all, the more people you involve in any business venture, the more complications you will run into regarding their involvement in the day-to-day operations of your company and if the investors are not satisfied with your performance, you can end up paying large legal fees for lawsuits which might put your company into a financial crisis. If you start an LLC, though, the assets you have that are separate from the LLC cannot be taken from you.

Financing: Many real estate speculators leverage themselves with the bank to buy properties they could never pay for, then turn around and sell them to see a nice return inside of six months or a year. If the truth be told, most real estate speculators are in the speculative game for the short-term turnaround. I personally lean towards the longer-term (2-3 years), using mostly cash because I work in many far-flung places for several different parties, but there is nothing wrong with either approach.

If you can swing the payments for a loan for about six months in an area where you are confident you can sell the property in that span of time for a nice return on your investment, investigate your ability to do so. Talk to ALL of the banks in your area in order to get the lowest interest percentage possible, and make sure you can get a loan with no prepayment penalties, because you will want to prepay it.

(The downside of leveraging yourself on vacant land or a house is that you may not be able to sell the property in the time you anticipated, in which case you will be stuck with payments you hadn't thought you would have to pay. Real estate is, after all, a hard asset and might not be able to be liquidated for some time. Take your time looking at the real estate market of the area and the different loans available to you.)

Getting a loan to buy land can be tricky in certain areas. Often if the area's real estate is showing a fair degree of value appreciation, the banks will be the first ones to get wind of it and they'll have a special speculator interest rate which is a few percentage points above the regular interest rate for land to buy and build. If you're lucky, you will have chosen an area where the banks are not yet offering speculator loans.

Chapter 8: Buying the Land:

If you have your real estate license, you have several options available to you during the purchase of property. You might be able to pay a lower commission to the agent you're working with, and of course, if you are buying a piece of unlisted property that you went out and found on your own, you can keep the commission and fill out the paperwork yourself (after properly disclosing to the seller in the appropriate ways that you're a real estate agent).

Your previous research should have left you with a good sense of what property values are in the area, so you should be able to somewhat accurately price real estate. If you're committed to buying a property, it is a good idea to get an appraisal so that you will have a second, more accurate opinion on the market value of the property. Professional appraisers will be listed in the yellow pages for your area and like any service you should shop around for the best price.

When deciding to buy, ALWAYS GET TITLE INSURANCE. This can save you money and embarrassment in the long run, because title insurance protects you from any liens (property tax, mechanics, or other) that may have been put on the property.

If you buy a house or land without getting title insurance, there is the possibility that you will run into trouble. For instance, situations sometimes occur where a house was built completely on credit and never paid off by the owner before being sold for full price. If that happens, a mechanics lien might be placed on the property if the owner didn't pay the builders. Then, THE NEW OWNER HAS TO PAY THE COST OF THE HOUSE'S CONSTRUCTION, OR THE HOUSE WILL BE SEIZED.

Don't let that happen to you. Always get title insurance.

Title insurance also will usually uncover any occurrences of pre-sold timber or mineral rights. Sometimes a land owner will sell the trees on his property before he lists it, knowing full well that potential purchasers will view and walk the property before the trees are cut, hoping they won't find out about the pre-sold timber rights until after the property's sale. While this is illegal, and it's the job of the listing agent to disclose an event like this, it can and does happen.

Title insurance also helps protect the buyer in circumstances where the seller sells a piece of property that isn't his in the first place. People have been known to pretend they own property and then "sell" it with a quitclaim deed.

Deeds:

Of any deed, a QUITCLAIM deed offers the least amount of protection to the buyer. It is used when transferring or conveying property from one party to another without representation or warranties, i.e. generally used in "AS IS" sales.

A quitclaim deed essentially says, "If I have any claim to this property (and I'm not saying I do) I agree to transfer it to you. I guarantee nothing about this property, its' title, or my ownership of it. But I welcome your money in exchange for this paper."

In other words, a quitclaim deed only has limited uses, and you don't need to know any of them here. Just know that you should usually not deal with quitclaim deeds to acquire real estate, and certainly never with someone you don't know. As I said before, quitclaim deeds have been used by criminals to buy and sell property that isn't theirs.

The most commonly used deed is the WARRANTY deed. The Warranty deed "warrants" that the property is being transferred with good title (i.e. without encumbrance except those that are filed on record).

<u>The best thing you can do for yourself when buying property is to buy title insurance and to go through a reputable real estate office.</u>

I won't go into the specifics of the questions you need to ask when buying a piece of property (vacant land or house) because every situation in every state is different, but just make sure that you consult with your CPA (Certified Public Accountant) and a title insurance representative, or even a lawyer. If you have received your real estate license or training for that state, you will better know the intricacies and details involved in land purchases there.

I will say, though, that it can often be a good idea to leave yourself an "out," in your offer so that you aren't obligated to buy a property you weren't informed fully about. People I have known have used contingencies like, "Subject to financing," in the offer because the word "financing" doesn't necessarily mean financing from the bank, it can just mean that you realized that you didn't want to spend that much money from your savings account.

Once you've negotiated a good price and covered all of the details, you can start having fun with your new property.

Chapter 9: Helping your property values:

Once you've bought a piece of vacant land, there are several relatively inexpensive things you can do to it that will help boost its market value. Market value is subjective, and the selling price of a property will depend mostly on the emotional response of the person looking at it. This is why it is possible to boost the value of a property just by making it look a little bit more attractive.

Subdividing:

If you acquired a larger piece of property, you can sometimes get a surveyor to divide it into smaller parcels. In my experience, a smaller lot that is in a desirable area can often cost just as much as a forty-acre parcel nearby. This is an occurrence similar to buying items retail versus wholesale. If you *do* acquire a large piece, it will cost some money to hire the surveyor and develop a new plat of the property, but in the long run it could be worth it. In other words, if you buy a forty-acre parcel for $40,000 and divide it into four, ten acre lots, you might be able to get close to the original $40,000 for each lot if the lots are nice, and depending on the area.

Docks:

If your land is on some sort of waterway, whether it be a creek, river, lake, or ocean, you might be able to construct a dock that will raise the value of the property much more than what you paid for it. I have seen $8,000 docks that automatically, once they were installed, boost the value of the property $50,000 or more. Docks can be an efficient way of boosting your property values on water.

Clearing Brush:

Making your property look clean and appealing to the largest number of people is always a plus, and it can be kind of fun if you enjoy getting your hands dirty. I know that I would rather look at and consider buying a piece of property that I could walk or drive through without much trouble. In fact, I once refused to consider buying a cheap, two acre piece of property in an area that was doing 25% annually because I couldn't get through to see the beach. And I'm a professional who shouldn't care about inconveniences (the land was sweltering and buggy with razor-sharp foliage), so imagine what the average buyer who makes decisions mostly based on emotions or frustrations would turn down! Rent a Bobcat, buy a machete, and clear your land. But leave the trees! Trees add aesthetic appeal that you don't want to lose.

You can also landscape on a small scale, if that's in your nature. Remember that you are appealing to the emotions of a potential purchaser, so if you are able to plant tulips, a garden, add a birdbath, or create a small, meditative sitting area where the agent and buyer can sit and talk, those are relatively inexpensive ways to make your asking price seem more valid as long as they aren't too invasive on the general nature of the property.

Driveways:

Driveways can be as cheap as you want them to be. They can be made of several truckloads of sand, if you want. You could dump gravel or crushed rock for a driveway. Some property owners in coastal towns even use the shells of mollusks as road fill. You could even pave a driveway, but of course, that's fairly expensive and you'll never know if the future buyer wants to put his house where the driveway ends. Usually, gravel or crushed rock is sufficient, and it shouldn't cost much more that a few thousand dollars while making the place look fairly nice and accessible.

Dredging:

I personally bought a two acre piece of property on a channel leading to a huge, beautiful lake in Minnesota. The channel hasn't been dredged in about fifteen years and it's impossible to get a boat into my shoreline. I found out before I purchased it that if I spend anywhere from $3,000 to $4,000 to dredge the channel, I can see an automatic property value escalation in the neighborhood of 30%. And this isn't a cheap piece of property, so that's several tens of thousands of dollars. Check with your state's environmental departments before doing anything, though, because as I said before, wetlands and marshes are a highly protected kind of land.

Writing Articles, Getting the Word Out:

You can always attempt to increase the visibility of the area where you bought property by writing an article with pictures for vacation magazines, airline magazines, online travel sites, or the vacation section of a metropolitan newspaper. It's hard to tell how much and how quickly this sort of marketing helps your property values, but it certainly doesn't hurt. Think about your audience when you write it, and bring to light all the areas' attractions, whether they have access to ski areas, a beautiful lake, good restaurants and shopping, a fine casino or hotel, whitewater rafting, historical sites, etc. Bring the best aspects of the place to the page and try to get it published somewhere. People *do* make vacation decisions based on what they read. I have even heard of some heavy-hitters commissioning documentaries for growing resort areas. Visibility comes in all forms.

Building Structures:

DON'T BUILD A HOUSE ON YOUR LAND!!!! Some people think that building a house or cabin on a piece of land is a good way to boost their property values, but a piece of land with a structure on it will only reflect the value of the land and the cost of the house's construction. Additionally, everyone's tastes are different, and the size and layout of the structure will limit the number of people who would want that kind of building. Vacant land is limitless in its' possibilities for a potential buyer and it's always cheaper for you. Land rarely depreciates in value, whereas structures always depreciate with age. From a sheerly financial perspective, building a house or cabin is a bad idea and incurs additional costs like insurance, maintenance, as well as *reducing your profit margin.*

The only time when building a house on your land can be beneficial (if you're not a professional builder who does it for a living) is when you claim it as a homestead and use it as *your primary residence,* spending at least six months and a day there per year for a minimum of two years. Using the house as a primary residence can open you up to the possibility of getting a $250,000 capital gains exclusion for a single person and up to $500,000 for a married couple. I'll talk briefly about this in the next chapter.

Chapter 10: Selling Your Property:

Once you have waited long enough to "reach your numbers," it's time to sell.

In order to see a fair and accurate sales price for your property, you will probably need to list for a price above the appraised value for the property. Once you go too high, however, you shrink the amount of people potentially interested in the property, and you lower your own standards so that you begin to "fish for suckers."

Author's Note: Although I can't blame anyone for trying to get as much money as possible out of their land, I HATE running across properties that are listed for double or triple the comparables. It's insulting to see property erroneously listed that high and the market will probably pass it by, anyway.

I personally recommend that you list your property with a well-respected, well-known real estate office in the town where the property is, instead of doing a For Sale By Owner. Their office will help you to price the property reasonably, in addition to allowing your property to be seen by a wider array of potential purchasers. If you have chosen the right area in the first place, the area will see a significant amount of out-of-towners visiting, leading to people unfamiliar with the region looking for qualified help at the local real estate offices and their internet web sites. Real estate offices get more calls, walk-ins, and website hits per day than you will have drive-by's in a week with your FSBO sign in the yard. It's probably best to list your property with a well-known, well-respected agency if you care about a relatively quick and painless sale.

Always list near the beginning of the tourist season. If you list your property out of season, you might feel the psychological pressure of not having anyone interested in it for a very long time, making you more prone to lowering your asking price when you do get an offer. We're all human. It happens.

Capital Gains:

If you bought a property with a house and have used it as a principal residence, you are allowed to sell it every two years and exclude your capital gains up to $250,000 for a single person and up to $500,000 for a married couple. Some people think that this is a once-in-a-lifetime exclusion, but that's not the case. As long as it's your principal residence, you may get this exclusion every two years. Ask your CPA about this possibility.

1031 Exchange:

The IRS allows a sale-and-purchase type transaction to be turned into an exchange. This allows owners of certain types of property to sell their property and buy other similar, like-kind property without paying the capital gains tax.

The 1031 exchange essentially defers capital gains throughout certain types of transactions until a later date, and it can be applied to real estate.

It gets quite complicated, though, so check with your CPA about the feasibility of the 1031 exchange.

Chapter 11: Final Advice and Miscellany

As in anything, chance can work with you or against you. There are problems you might have with buying, owning, and selling land that you will never have been able to anticipate. For instance, an economy where everyone is scrambling for cash can reduce the demand for hard assets and potentially lose you money because you might need cash too. Pay attention to the economy.

I recently heard about a large region in the Southwest where scientists are beginning to think a 1,000 year drought is beginning. I have no idea how much this will affect property values or the appeal of the area, but as an individual I am hedging my bets by buying in different regions.

The same is true with flooding and rising ocean levels. Beach erosion on the oceans is already a big issue in certain coastal towns of America, and if a hurricane hits one of those places, certain unprotected properties will disappear. It happens all the time. Losing your property to the ocean will of course hurt your property values.

Just for kicks, take a look at how much the ice-caps have melted in the past fifty years, project the appropriate level of melting forward ten or twenty years, and calculate the amount of valuable beach front property American homeowners and investors will lose in the future. We can't count on losing beach front property, however, since retaining walls are a big business already (and the entire country of Holland is proof that humanity can withstand the weight of oceans), but the reason I mention this is to make you aware that global or local problems you never saw coming can emerge that impact real estate in any given locale.

Certain parts of Louisiana are sinking anywhere from seven inches to a foot every decade. Some have theorized that the reason for the sinking is because of the depletion of underground natural gas and oil, but whatever the reason, I'll bet nobody who bought land in those areas ever counted on eventually living below sea level.

Using my methods for making wise decisions about speculative real estate only goes so far. "Acts of God" will always exist, but insurance can sometimes help lessen the blow. But it's almost always impossible to insure vacant land.

6 Ways to be a Good Speculator:
Real estate is complicated. There are many occasions that can lead to consequences you never planned on or were capable of envisioning.

More than anything, you need to have a good head on your shoulders to succeed in speculative real estate. Unfortunately, common sense is not something that this book teaches, and if you don't have it, you might encounter troubles with locals or the law.

It will help you to pay close attention to the following advice:

1. Take an appropriate and well-taught real estate class (Ask around. The teacher either makes the material accessible and fun, or not.). Going through a real estate course will take some time, but I GUARANTEE you will benefit exponentially from the information you receive. It will familiarize you with real estate terminology and real estate law. If you get your license, you will have the potential to earn referral fees or commissions on many sales or purchases you arrange. It can also give you a professional-looking acronym behind your name so that you can look cool on your business card.

2. Stay honest. Clinton's Whitewater scandal took place because people were accused of being unscrupulous. Keep your dealings honest or you could end up involved in lawsuits. Know the law and treat it with respect.

3. Watch out for crooked Real Estate Agents, Brokers, or For Sale By Owners (FSBO's). As in any industry, criminals also exist in real estate. Only by knowing what you're doing and knowing what questions to ask (via your real estate license classes) can you really be prepared to tell who is

lying and who is telling the truth. Be careful and QUESTION EVERYTHING. And never give FSBO's full price for their property. They often get unfairly greedy and that's why they're often not listing with any REALTORS® who tell them to lower their sky-high prices.

4. Always get title insurance, get an appraisal before you buy, and don't buy property via a quitclaim deed.

5. Don't put all your eggs in one basket. As with any investment strategy, you limit your risk by diversifying the places where you put your money. You shouldn't put all of your savings in speculative real estate, because there are never guarantees on value appreciation and hard assets can sometimes be quite difficult to sell. Diversifying your assets generally helps to insulate you from the unexpected.

6. DON'T GET EMOTIONALLY ATTACHED TO YOUR PROPERTY! You are doing what you're doing to make money, not to fall in love. You may certainly enjoy it while you have it, but you won't make ANY money on it if you don't sell it. Remember that.

Conclusion:

I have intentionally avoided naming specific places in America where I and my clients have real estate investments that will see large returns in a few short years. To name those specific college towns and resort areas would, I believe, be unprofessional and could lead you astray. After all, if I wanted to boost my own property values and those of my clients, what better way to attract people to the area than to mention those specific places in a book? And if enough people read a book like that, it could inadvertently create real estate bubbles that could burst and drag down individuals, families, and businesses. That is why I have withheld mentioning the areas where my clients and I are invested.

Additionally, most suitable areas for real estate speculation before 2009 do not need my help to succeed. The shifting of populations is a real generational trend with real value appreciation and it is much larger than just myself and my clients. This national shift to exurbia will continue to expand and gain converts as time goes on, as 401k's mature, as investors infuse capital in both liquid and hard assets, as cities become less desirable, as Baby Boomers buy second homes and start retiring, as Baby Boomers inherit trillions from their parents, as individuals, families and businesses move to the exurbs for the lower taxes and the favorable costs of living, and as the internet continues to help home-based businessees operate from anywhere in America. 2009 is when this head of steam is expected to slow, even though the Fifth American Population Shift will continue until 2020 and beyond.

In conclusion, start doing research on your weekends into real estate in these areas. Take a real estate course and if you feel it's right for you, get your license. Investigate creative financing options, set up LLC's or partnerships, and learn the tricks of the trade.

But most importantly, don't forget that there is fun to be had and money to be made in these beautiful, dynamic regions of our incredible nation. These areas will grow and appreciate in value with or without you.

Always do your research.

Good luck.

Section II:

Real Estate
Workbook

Notes/ Properties/ Journal

Notes/ Properties/ Journal

Notes/ Properties/ Journal

Grids for sales price (acreage, lots, houses)/ years

Grids for sales price (acreage, lots, houses)/ years

Grids for sales price (acreage, lots, houses)/ years

Grids for sales price (acreage, lots, houses)/ years

Grids for sales price (acreage, lots, houses)/ years

Contact list

_____

_____

_____

_____

_____

_____

_____

_____

_____

_____

_____

_____

_____

_____

_____

_____

_____

Contact list

_____

_____

_____

_____

_____

_____

_____

_____

_____

_____

_____

_____

_____

_____

About the Author:

For the last ten years, Andrew R. Garvey has been an advisory director of Builders, Inc., a real estate development and management company based out of Wichita, KS. He currently researches and recommends speculative real estate across America for his clients and business interests.

You may send your comments about the book to
AndrewGarvey@hotmail.com